An Introduction to the
British Seashore

A Photographic Guide

Sally Morgan

WAYLAND

First published in Great Britain in 2006 by Wayland, an imprint of Hachette
Children's Books

Hachette Children's Books
338 Euston Road, London NW1 3BH

Editor: Victoria Brooker
Senior Design Manager: Rosamund Saunders
Designer: Janice Utton

Printed and bound in China

British Library Cataloguing in Publication Data
Morgan, Sally
   An introduction to the British seashore: a photographic
   guide
   1.Seashore animals - Great Britain - Juvenile literature
   2.Seashore plants - Great Britain - Juvenile literature
   I.Title
   578.7'699'0941

ISBN-10: 0-7502-4847-5
ISBN-13: 978-0-7502-4847-1

Cover photograph: the shells of a variety of molluscs, including mussels,
periwinkles and topshells, in a rock pool.

Photo credits: Ecoscene cover and 5 Andrew Brown; 8, 9 Simon Grove;
14, 17, 29 (both) Chinch Gryniewicz; 28 Angela Hampton; 12, 16 Kevin King;
21 (both), 25 John Liddiard; 22 Michael Maconachie; 6, 7 (top), 10, 11, 18
Sally Morgan; 24 Steve Newman; 27 Peter Tatton; title page and 4
John Wilkinson: **Premaphotos** 7 (bottom), 13, 15, 20 Ken Preston-Mafham;
19, 23, 26 Rod Preston-Mafham.

Contents

The seashore

The seashore is a fascinating place that is full of wildlife. There are long sandy beaches, muddy estuaries where rivers meet the sea and shores covered in rocks. The seashore is a changing habitat and the plants and animals that are found there are used to living in a place where the sea level rises and falls twice a day.

The tides are vitally important to everything that lives on the shore. As the tides change, the conditions for the animals on the shore change too.

Their survival is linked to these changes. There are two high tides and two low tides every day, with about six hours between a high tide and a low tide. At high tide the waves come right up the shore and everything is covered by salt water. At low tide, the whole of the shore is exposed to the sun, wind and rain.

Scientists who study the seashore divide it into three areas, the upper, middle and lower shore. Plants and animals that live on the upper shore

◄ *Rock pools can be seen on a rocky shore at low tide.*

are used to being out of water for long periods of time. In contrast, the lower shore is exposed for a short time and the animals and plants that live here are less able to survive being out of water. When the animals are covered by water they come out of their hiding places and start feeding. When the tide goes out they retreat into cracks, under seaweed or into rock pools (small pools of water trapped between rocks) and wait until the water returns.

Many different types of animals and seaweeds can be found on the shore. There are sea anemones, worms and crustaceans such as crabs and prawns. There are many different types of molluscs (the animals which have a shell) for example mussels, periwinkles and limpets. There are spiny-skinned animals called echinoderms such as starfish and sea urchins. All these animals are invertebrates – animals that do not have a backbone. But there are some vertebrates too, such as small fish that can be found in rock pools.

In this book you will read about some of the common animals and seaweeds that are found on the seashores around Britain. You will learn how to identify them, their behaviour and the types of seashore on which they occur.

Seashores can be dangerous
Take care. Shores can be dangerous places and it is not safe for you to visit them on your own.

▲ *The shells of a variety of molluscs, including mussels, periwinkles and top shells have been washed up on this shore.*

Seaweeds

Seaweeds are plant-like organisms found on shores, especially rocky shores. They belong to a group of organisms called algae. A seaweed consists of a leaf-like frond and a stem called a stipe. At the end of the stipe is a holdfast which acts like a root, gripping the rock so the seaweed is not carried away by the tide. Many seaweeds are slippery because they are covered in mucus. This is a jelly-like substance produced by the seaweed that stops the frond from drying out when it is out of water.

Some seaweeds are tough and can survive being battered by the waves. Others grow on sheltered shores where the waves are smaller. The larger seaweeds are usually found on the lower shore where they are not out of water for very long, if at all. On some sheltered shores there is a dense forest of seaweeds growing in the water below the low tide mark.

There are three main types of seaweed: green, red and brown. About 800 species of seaweed are found on the British coast.

▼ *Rock pools are good places to look for seaweeds as you can see them in the water rather than flopped on the rocks. This makes them easier to identify.*

GREEN SEAWEEDS

Latin name: *Ulva lactuca* (Sea lettuce)

Size: fronds up to 30 cm in length

Type of seashore: rocky shores

Position on shore: upper shore, particularly where streams empty onto beaches

There are two common types of green seaweed on the shore: sea lettuce and enteromorpha. Sea lettuce grows up to 30 cm across. Its frond is broad and thin and it flops over the rocks when the tide is out. It is easily damaged by waves, so it is mostly found on sheltered shores. The fronds of enteromorpha look like paper-thin, long, green strips. This seaweed is often seen in rock pools high up the shore. Green seaweeds are common in places where streams run down on to the shore. Often these seaweeds cover the rocks in a slippery carpet.

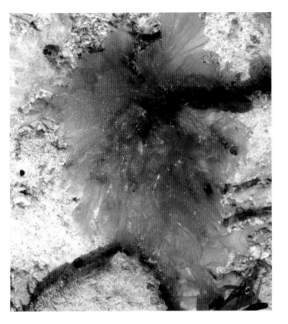

◀ *Sea lettuce is very easy to identify as it looks like a piece of salad lettuce. However, it is very slimy to the touch.*

RED SEAWEEDS

Latin name: *Chondrus crispus* (Carragheen)

Size: 7-15 cm long

Type of seashore: rocky shores

Position on shore: lower to middle shore

Red seaweeds tend to be smaller than brown seaweeds (see pages 8-9) and they are found in deeper water. Purple laver forms into large, thin sheets in winter. In many parts of Wales and Ireland it is collected and boiled until tender and used to make laver bread, which is like a seaweed pancake. The laver bread is fried and served with bacon for breakfast.

Carragheen, or Irish moss, is a red seaweed that is found on rocks and in rock pools. When it is covered by water it has a purple appearance. It is rich in a substance called gelatine which is used to set jellies and other desserts.

◀ *This is a branching red seaweed. The edges of the seaweed appear purple when underwater.*

BROWN SEAWEEDS

The most common seaweeds on rocky shores are brown seaweeds. They are found all over the shore, right up to the high tide mark.

Spiral wrack is found higher up the shore than the other brown seaweeds and it can grow up to 40 cm in length. It is named after the way its fronds are twisted into a spiral so the seaweed does not lie completely flat at low tide. It can cope with being out of water for long periods of time.

The channel wrack is found high on the shore. This seaweed can survive longer out of water than any other seaweed. Often it looks shrivelled and black but it recovers when covered by water. It gets its name from the way the frond rolls inwards creating a channel that traps water.

Bladder wrack or popweed is a brown seaweed that is found attached to rocks on the middle of rocky shores and in some estuaries. It gets its name from tough, air-filled pods or bladders along its fronds. These bladders help the fronds to float, keeping the seaweed in the sunlight.

▼ *The fronds of spiral wrack are twisted so the seaweed does not lie completely flat on the rocks at low tide.*

Another type of brown seaweed is egg or knotted wrack. This seaweed has bladders which are found in a line down the middle of the frond. The fronds of egg wrack grow up to two metres or more in length.

Egg wrack does not live on shores where there are large waves which would smash onto the rocks and damage the fronds. It tends to be found on the middle shore of sheltered rocky seashores. It can live for 15 years or more whilst other wracks survive for about three years. The age of this seaweed can be estimated by counting the large bladders along a frond, as one is formed each year.

A number of large brown seaweeds, known as oarweeds or kelps, can be found below the low tide mark. Sugar kelp or sea belt grows up to 2 metres in length. Each frond looks like a long piece of ribbon with a frilled edge. The holdfast on the sugar kelp is branched but very small in comparison with the other oarweeds. The stipe is thin and flexible and this allows the seaweed to go limp at low tide so that it lies flat in the water and does not dry out.

Tangleweed is another large seaweed, it grows to about 3 metres in length. The frond is divided lengthways into lots of strips. The holdfast is large and very branched to give a strong attachment to rock. Like sugar kelp, the stipe of tangleweed is flexible so at low tide the plant goes limp and lies flat.

▲ *Tangleweed is only seen at low tide when its long fronds lie over the rocks. A holdfast can be seen in the middle of the photograph.*

Periwinkles

Type of animal: mollusc

Shell: single, spiral shell

Size: from 2 mm (small periwinkle) to 6 cm (edible periwinkle)

Type of seashore: rocky shores

Position on shore: upper, middle and lower shores

Periwinkles are small molluscs that are found all over rocky shores. They are related to the snails that you see in the garden and park. Periwinkles are not the only molluscs on the shore.

There are whelks, limpets, topshells, razor shells and mussels to name a few. Molluscs are animals that have shells. Their hard shell protects them from waves, sun, wind and attack by other animals. Some molluscs have a single shell. The shell may be cone-shaped like limpets, or in the form of a spiral like periwinkles. Mussels, razor shells and cockles are called bivalves because they have two shells that are joined together.

There are four types of periwinkle found on rocky shores. The small periwinkle is the smallest, just a few

▼ *The flat periwinkle is well camouflaged on bladder wrack because it looks similar to one of the bladders of the seaweed.*

millimetres in length. It is found at the top of the shore which is covered by water just a few times a year, during exceptionally high tides or in rough weather. It is found in crevices that stay moist. It feeds on lichens, plant-like organisms that grow over the surface of the rocks of the upper shore. The rough periwinkle is found towards the top of the middle shore. Its shell is coloured yellow, orange or brown and it feels rough to the touch.

The flat periwinkle is not actually flat but rounded in shape. Its shell is about a centimetre long. It can be seen in a variety of colours, ranging from olive-green, brown and black to yellow and orange. It is commonly found on the middle shore where it feeds on bladder wrack. When the tide is out flat periwinkles crawl under seaweeds so that they do not dry out.

The edible or common periwinkle is the largest of the periwinkles, growing up to 6 cm in length. Its shell is dark with lighter bands. It is found on the middle and lower shore where it feeds on microscopic algae that cover the rocks. It scrapes its tongue, called a radula, across the rock surface. The radula is covered in tiny teeth. The periwinkle's heavy shell protects it from drying out and from wave damage. Edible periwinkles cluster together in cracks in the rocks or under seaweeds when the tide goes out. They produce a sticky substance that they use to glue themselves to the rock. Then they close the openings of their shells so no water escapes.

▲ *If you look into cracks in the rocks at the top of the shore you may see many small periwinkles squeezed into the spaces, sheltering from the sun.*

Limpets

Latin name: *Patella vulgaris* (common limpet)	
Type of animal: mollusc	
Shell: single, dome-shaped	
Size: up to 5 cm across	
Type of seashore: rocky shores	
Position on shore: middle to lower shore	

Limpets are common on rocky shores and are very easy to identify. They have a single domed shell. There are several species of limpet including the common, blue-rayed, keyhole and tortoiseshell limpets. The common limpet grows slowly, reaching about 5 cm across at the base within four years. Limpets are important seashore herbivores (animals that feed on plants), feeding on microscopic algae on the rocks. Limpets breed in autumn by releasing eggs into the water. The larvae (young limpets) float in the water for about 10 days and then settle on rocks when their shells start to form.

When the tide is out, limpets survive by clamping firmly to the rock so they do not dry out. As a limpet clamps down, it rotates its shell and this grinds into the rock to create a good fit. It moves back to exactly the same place on the rock each day and when it dies a scar is left on the rock.

Other species of limpet are smaller than the common limpet, growing to about 1.5 cm across. Young blue-rayed limpets have a shell with three blue lines across it. They are found among kelp (see page 9) on which they feed. The keyhole limpet is named after the small hole in the top of its shell. Tortoiseshell limpets have flatter, brown and white shells.

▼ *These limpets are clamped firmly to the rock as they are exposed by the tide. Shores where there are large numbers of limpets tend to have less seaweed attached to the rocks as the limpets eat the young seaweeds.*

Top shells

◀ *Top shells are found close to brown seaweeds which they feed on.*

Type of animal: mollusc	
Shell: single, cone-shaped spiral	
Size: up to 1.5 cm wide and tall	
Type of seashore: rocky shores	
Position on shore: middle and lower shore	

Top shells are colourful molluscs that are found on rocky shores around Britain. Their name comes from the fact that their shell looks a bit like a child's spinning top. They are herbivores and they like to feed on the seaweeds such as bladder and serrated wracks. In doing so they help to control the amount of these brown seaweeds growing on a shore. The most common species is the painted top shell but there are several other species including the purple, grooved and grey top shells.

The top shells have a cone-shaped shell with a flat base. Often the surface is worn showing a layer of mother-of-pearl underneath. Many top shells have a small hole in their shell which can be seen when they are turned over. This hole leads to a hollow spiral that runs through the centre of the shell.

The purple top shell is probably the most widespread species in Britain. It has colourful purple bands across its greenish shell. Its shell reaches 1.5 cm in height and width.

The painted top shell has a yellow or pink shell with colourful streaks of red. Its shell is slightly larger than the purple top shell, growing up to 3 cm high and wide. The shell of the grey top shell is 12 mm tall and is pale grey with dark grey stripes.

Most top shells are found on the middle and lower shores. The purple top shell is abundant across the middle seashore where it is found on the brown seaweeds. Painted top shells are common on the lower shore. The grey top shell spends most of its life underwater so it is found near or below the low tide mark.

Whelks

Latin name:	*Nucella lapillus* (dog whelk)
Type of animal:	mollusc
Shell:	single, spiral
Size:	up to 3 cm
Type of seashore:	rocky
Position on shore:	middle to lower shore

Whelks have a shell with a distinct groove at the bottom. They also have a structure called a siphon which is a tube that extends out from the shell. The siphon is used to detect food.

One of the most common molluscs on the rocky shore is the dog whelk. It is about 3 cm in length with a long spiral shell. The shell is mostly off white but it can be brown, yellow or orange. In some places there are purple dog whelks. They are active predators, preying mostly on acorn barnacles (see page 18) and mussels (see page 16). They attack barnacles by boring a hole through their shell while they force the two shells of the mussel apart. Then they suck out the body of the animal. Dog whelks are found on exposed rocky shores where there is not much seaweed but plenty of barnacles and mussels to eat.

The netted dog whelk has a shell covered with a network of ridges and grooves. This dog whelk is found on sandy shores where it feeds mostly on food particles in the water and the rotting bodies of animals.

Dog whelks lay their eggs on the underside of rocks. The eggs are laid together in a capsule. The capsule is a vase-shaped structure, about 8 mm high and yellow in colour and sticks to the rock. Tiny larvae hatch from the eggs and float in the sea. Eventually the larvae settle on a beach and develop into adult dog whelks.

The common whelk or buckle is the largest snail in Britain, growing up to 15 cm in length. It is found on the lower shore of sandy or gravel beaches.

▲ *These yellow dog whelks are feeding on mussels. The mussels cannot escape as they are fixed to the rock. It may take a day for a dog whelk to eat one barnacle and a week for it to eat a mussel.*

Cockles

Type of animal:	mollusc
Shell:	two, hinged together
Size:	up to 5 cm across
Type of seashore:	sandy shores, estuaries
Position on shore:	lower shore

Cockles can be found on many sandy shores and estuaries where they live just under the surface. They need to live in clean sand so they are found lower down the shore where the tides keep the sand clean.

Cockles are bivalves which means they have two shells that are hinged together. They feed by filtering plankton from the water. Cockles are preyed on by oystercatchers, shore crabs, shrimps and flatfish. People eat them too, and collect large numbers of them. The edible cockle has an off-white, yellowish or brown shell with prominent ribs. It is also possible to see growth lines across the surface of the shell. This cockle is found on the middle to lower shore, where it burrows into soft sand and muddy gravel to depths of less than 5 cm. It is often found in huge numbers in estuaries. The prickly cockle is similar but, as the name suggests, the outside of its shell has spiny ribs.

The rate at which the cockle grows varies through the year. In winter there is very little growth but there is a lot of growth in summer and this creates bands on the shell. These bands can be used to tell the age of a cockle. Most cockles live for two to four years, but some may live for as long as nine years.

◀ *When covered with water, these cockles open their shells slightly and feed by drawing water into their bodies and removing the food particles.*

Mussels

Latin name: *Mytilus edulis* (common mussel)

Type of animal: mollusc

Shell: two, hinged together

Size: up to 10 cm in length

Type of seashore: rocky shores

Position on shore: upper to lower shore

Like cockles, mussels are bivalves (molluscs with two shells). These molluscs do not move around like limpets. Instead they stay in one place on the rocks, held firmly in position by sticky threads which they produce. Usually they are found clustered together. Their shells give the mussels protection. When the tide goes out they are exposed, their shells clamp together to prevent water escaping.

Mussels can survive on very exposed shores where there are large waves.

Mussels are filter feeders. This means that they draw water into their body through a gap between their two shells and sieve tiny animals from the water. However, they can only feed when they are covered by water. Water is drawn in through tubes called siphons and passed through the gills where food particles are trapped and eaten. Mussels living higher up the shore tend to be smaller as they are out of the water for longer, so cannot feed for as long as those living on the lower shore.

There are three types of mussel on British seashores; common, horse and fan mussels. The one that is most likely to be seen is the common mussel. This has two dark blue shells that grow up to 10 cm in length.

▼ *Common mussels are preyed upon by dog whelks, starfish, shore crabs, oystercatchers and other birds. People like to eat them too!*

Razor shells

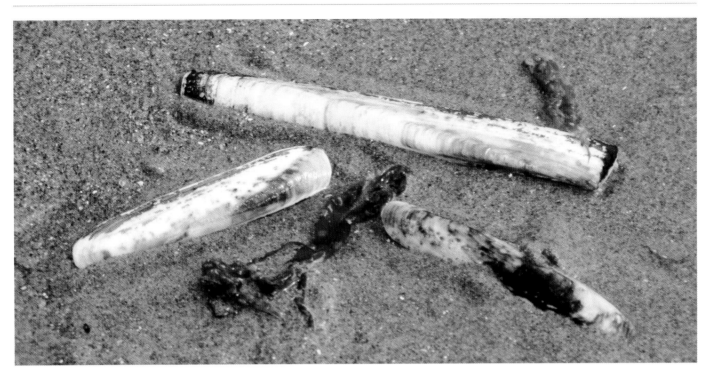

Latin name:	*Ensis ensis* (curved razor shell)
Type of animal:	mollusc
Shell:	two, hinged together
Size:	up to 13 cm in length
Type of seashore:	muddy and sandy shores
Position on shore:	lower shore

One mollusc that is very easy to identify is the razor shell, a type of bivalve. Each of its shells is slightly curved and grows up to 13 cm in length. They get their name from the shape of their shells which is a bit like that of a cut-throat razor. Each shell is smooth on the outside and whitish in colour with vertical and horizontal red-brown and purple-brown markings. The inside of the shell is white with a purple tinge. There are several common species of razor shell and they only differ slightly by the size and shape of the shell.

Living razor shells are rarely seen as they live in burrows in the sand but empty shells are regularly washed up on sandy beaches. The presence of razor shells in sand is indicated by keyhole-shaped openings. When the tide is in the razor shells move to the top of their burrow to feed and when the tide goes out they move deeper into the sand. They have a muscular foot that can dig quickly into the sand. The only way to see a living razor shell is to dig it up. However, this can be quite difficult as they can move deeper into the sand faster than a person can dig.

Razor shells start to reproduce once they are about three years old. Breeding takes place during spring. The tiny larvae live in the plankton, where they float in the sea for around one month. Then they settle on the shore and grow into an adult razor shell. Razor shells live for about 10 years.

▲ *The empty shells of the razor shell are a common sight on sandy beaches.*

Barnacles

Latin name: *Balanus balanoides* (acorn barnacle)

Type of animal: crustacean

Size: from 1 to 10 cm

Type of seashore: rocky shores

Position on shore: middle and lower shore

Barnacles are crustaceans although they look more like tiny limpets. A crustacean is an animal that is covered in a heavy exoskeleton with legs that are jointed, for example shrimps, crabs and lobsters.

There are two types of barnacle on the seashore, acorn and goose barnacles. The most common is the acorn barnacle which is found in large numbers on rocks on the middle and lower shore. In some places there can be as many as 500 million acorn barnacles along one kilometre of rocky shore.

The acorn barnacle is just one centimetre across. It surrounds itself with armour plating made up of six outer plates and four smaller plates which join together to form a lid. This plating can have sharp edges and it can give you a nasty cut if you slip on barnacle-covered rocks. Inside there are six pairs of feathery legs. The plating allows the barnacle to survive being exposed for long periods. When the tide goes out, barnacles clamp their lids down tightly. When they are covered by water they open their lids and extend their legs to catch food in the water. One of the main predators of acorn barnacles is the dog whelk (see page 14).

The goose barnacle is less common. It is white or grey and it hangs from a tough stalk. It grows up to 10 cm in length. The name 'goose barnacle' comes from the animal's resemblance to a goose's head and neck.

▲ *Barnacles cannot move once they have settled on the rocks and made their armour plating. They may live for up to 12 years. When they die the empty shells remain on the rocks and often become homes for other animals such as small periwinkles.*

Sponges

Latin name: *Halichondria panacea*
(breadcrumb sponge)

Type of animal: sponge

Type of seashore: rocky shores

Position on shore: lower shore

Sponges are very simple animals as they are just a group of cells living together. They do not have any blood vessels or nerves seen in animals such as worms or insects. A sponge feeds by drawing water into its body through tiny holes and then removing any food particles. The water leaves the body through one large hole. The wall of the body is stiffened by tiny splinters which are often made from silica. Sponges have amazing powers of regeneration. In an experiment a sponge was forced through a fine mesh net. After a few hours the bits of sponge were seen to group together to form many new sponges.

There are about 250 different types of sponge found along the British coast. These sponges are much smaller than those found in warmer seas. Their shape and colour can be very variable so it is quite difficult to identify many of them without the help of a microscope.

Most sponges are found on the lower shore and are of the encrusting type, forming a crust-like growth over the surface of rocks. One of the most common sponges is the breadcrumb sponge. Its surface is smooth and there are volcano-shaped openings to let out water. In sheltered places it may be very thick, as much as 20 cm in places, and it can be several metres across. However, both its colour and shape vary greatly. If the sponge is exposed to light it is likely to be green but if it is growing in the shade it is yellow. The green colour is from thousands of tiny algae living inside the sponge. They provide food for the sponge and in return are protected by it. Algae need light to make their food so they are not found in sponges growing in shady places.

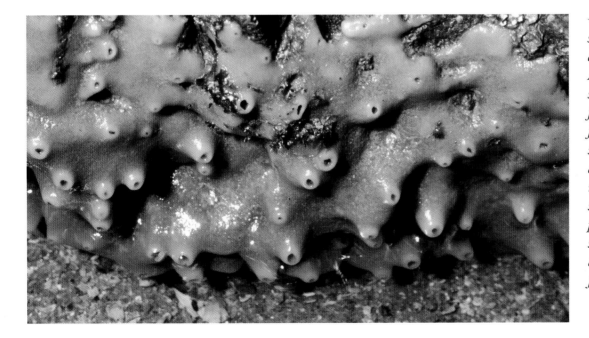

◀ *The breadcrumb sponge lives for about three years. Although it gets some protection from predators from the sharp splinters in its walls and from the unpleasant-tasting substances it produces, predators such as sea slugs and starfish still feed on it.*

Sea anemones

Sea anemones are animals that live on most rocky shores. They look a bit like flowers, hence they are often called the flower animals. There are about 40 different types of sea anemone living on British shores.

Sea anemones are cnidarians – simple animals consisting of a body shaped like a sac or bag and a ring of tentacles that surround the mouth. The tentacles are covered in sting cells which are used to stun or kill their prey, including small crabs, shrimps and fish. The prey is then carried to the mouth and passed into the middle of the body to be broken down. Sea anemones can move very slowly over

rocks and they will fight any other anemone that they meet for space.

The beadlet anemone is very common and it is found higher up the shore than other anemones. It is between 2 and 4 cm in height and is coloured red, green or brown. There is a ring of 24 blue spots beneath the tentacles. Each beadlet anemone has about 200 tentacles covered in sting cells. When the tide goes out the anemone pulls its tentacles inside its body and it looks like a blob of jelly. This helps to prevent water loss.

The dahlia anemone is the largest British anemone, growing up to 10 cm in height. It has up to 160 short, red

▼ *Sea anemones, such as this beadlet anemone, are attached to the rock and very difficult for predators to remove.*

and white banded tentacles. The rest of its body is often red with green or grey blotches. This anemone is found very firmly attached to rocks on the lower shore as it cannot survive being exposed for very long. However, it can pull in its tentacles when out of the water. It prefers shores where there is strong wave action.

The snakelocks anemone has long flowing tentacles and is usually bright green in colour, sometimes with purple tips to the tentacles. The green colour is due to the presence of algae. As in sponges, the presence of algae helps the sea anemone as the algae produce food while being protected by living inside the sea anemone. The algae need light so the snakelocks anemone is found in the sunniest rock pools. Unlike the other sea anemones, the snakelocks anemone cannot pull in its tentacles when exposed by the tide.

▲ The red and white banded tentacles of the dahlia anemone are covered in sting cells which are used to catch prey.

◄ The snakelocks anemone is found on the southern and western shores of Britain.

Crabs and prawns

Crabs and prawns are crustaceans. They are covered in a heavy external skeleton called an exoskeleton that protects the soft body inside. The exoskeleton is rigid so the animal cannot grow inside it. To become larger a crustacean has to cast off its old exoskeleton and grow bigger before the new exoskeleton underneath hardens. There are about 50 different types of crab as well as lobsters, prawns and shrimps living around Britain.

The shore crab is common on all types of shores, especially rocky ones. It is found on the middle to lower shore. The shore crab's flattened body is perfect for slipping under rocks and it can grow up to 8 cm across. The part of the exoskeleton that covers the back of the crab is called the carapace. It has five points on each side of its carapace which makes it easy to identify. This is an active crab that can scuttle sideways very quickly, sliding under seaweeds and rocks to escape from predators. Like all crabs the shore crab is a scavenger feeding on dead animals but it will also catch and kill small animals.

Two other types of crabs, the edible and the hermit crab can be found on British shores, especially rocky shores. The edible crab can grow up to 28 cm across, but those that are found on shores are rarely more than 10 cm

▼ *The shore crab is usually greenish brown in colour but those living on sandy beaches may be very pale.*

across. This is the type of crab that is sold in shops for people to eat. Its carapace has a 'pie-crust' edge, which looks like the wavy edge of a pie.

The hermit crab doesn't have a very hard shell so it uses other shells such as old whelk shells for protection. When threatened it retreats inside its shell, blocking the entrance with its large claws. Hermit crabs can grow up to 35 cm in length. As it gets larger it outgrows its shell and has to find a new one. It quickly pulls its body out of the old one and moves into the new one. Hermit crabs are found on the middle to lower part of the shore.

Shrimps and prawns have a body that looks as if it has been squashed from side to side. There are five pairs of slender legs, each of which ends in a small claw which is used to catch food. Shrimps and prawns look very similar and one way to tell them apart is to look at the snout that lies between the eyes. Prawns have a spiny snout whereas it is smooth or even absent in shrimps. The common prawn is found amongst seaweeds in rock pools. Its body is up to 10 cm long and is almost transparent.

The lobster is the largest crustacean living along British shores. It is found offshore along rocky coasts. Lobsters are blue-brown in colour. They can weigh up to 2 kg and grow to about 50 cm in length. Lobsters have five pairs of legs. The front pair is greatly enlarged to form large claws. Lobsters are nocturnal animals, coming out at night to hunt crabs, molluscs and other shore animals.

Echinoderms

Echinoderms are spiny-skinned animals such as starfish, sea urchins and brittlestars. Their bodies are supported by their spiny skeletons, which are made up of close-fitting plates that form a rigid shell. They also have lots of long, thin water-filled tube feet (see page 25), which help them to move and to grip prey.

There are seven species of starfish. The common starfish has five arms around a central disc. Common starfish can grow as large as 50 cm in diameter but most range between 10 and 30 cm. They are usually orange in colour but some are shades of brown or even violet. Not all starfish have five arms. Each species has a particular number, for example, one species of sunstar has 13 arms.

Starfish are predators and they move over the shore in search of prey, especially mussels and barnacles. They use their tube feet to grip their prey and to force open the shells of mussels. Once open, the starfish pours the contents of its stomach over its prey. This digests the body of their prey and then the starfish sucks up the remains.

Starfish can re-grow any arm that is broken off by a predator or by a strong wave. An arm that is pulled off may grow into a new starfish.

Sea urchins are shaped like a ball with lots of moveable spines. Their tube feet extend beyond the spines. Sea urchins move slowly on their

▲ *Starfish may be found on sandy and rocky shores, mostly on the lower shore and in deeper water.*

spines, gripping and pulling with their tube feet. They feed mostly on algae that covers the rocks but they will also feed on animals such as barnacles and sponges that are attached to the rocks. Sea urchins can be found in sheltered rock pools on the lower shore, hiding in crevices or under large stones.

The green sea urchin is a relatively small species of urchin, being just 5 cm across. It is green in colour while the tips of its spines are violet. Often it is camouflaged with bits of seaweed. The common sea urchin is much larger at 15 cm across. It is purple and red in colour.

Brittlestars look a bit like starfish but they have longer legs and a small body. Some are found on sandy shores where they bury themselves in the sand while others hide under stones or cling to seaweeds. As their name suggests, their arms are easily damaged but they can grow back.

The heart urchin, or sea potato, lives on sandy shores. It has a flatter shape than other sea urchins and it uses its small spines to bury itself deep in the sand when the tide goes out.

◀ *The tube feet of this sea urchin have tiny suckers at the end to help pull it along.*

Worms

Latin name: *Arenicola marina* (lugworm)	
Type of animal: segmented worm	
Size: 18-20 cm	
Type of seashore: sandy shores and estuaries	
Position on shore: lower shore	

Large worms can be found along sandy shores and on estuaries. However, many live in burrows in the mud so are difficult to spot.

Lugworms live in U-shaped burrows in sand and mud. Their cylindrical bodies are made up of sections called segments and 13 of these segments have gills that they use to absorb oxygen. They have a small head with no eyes. They reach up to 20 cm in length and range in colour from pink to green, brown and black. They feed by eating mud that they draw into their burrow.

The peacock worm is a long, slender fan worm that grows up to 30 cm in length. It lives in a smooth tube which it builds around its body using sand and mud. The tube protrudes up to 10 cm above the sea bed. There are about 100 orange and purple feathery tentacles at the head end. These worms can extend their tentacles to form a fan, which traps food floating in the water. When the worm is exposed at low tide or disturbed by a predator, it pulls its tentacles back into its tube.

The ragworm has a flattened body up to 20 cm in length. There are between 90 and 120 segments. Its head has two antennae and four pairs of tentacles. It lives in burrows and under stones along muddy shores.

▼ *A lugworm is rarely seen out of its burrow. You can find a burrow by looking for marks in the mud. One end of the burrow is marked by a pile of coiled mud, while the other end is a depression in the mud with a hole in the middle.*

Fish

◄ *This blenny is well camouflaged against the sandy background. Blennies grow to about 10 cm in length.*

Latin name: *Blennius pholis* (shanny)	
Type of animal: fish	
Size: 10 cm	
Type of seashore: mostly rocky shores	
Position on shore: rock pools on the middle to lower shore	

A number of different types of small fish are found along shores. Many live in rock pools where they are trapped until the tide returns. They include blennies, gobies, sea scorpions, clingfish and sand eels.

The shanny, or common blenny, is one of the most common rock pool fish. It has a single long dorsal fin on its back divided into two by a slight depression. There is a dark spot on the front of the dorsal fin. These fish do not have any scales. The shanny is unusual in that it can change the colour of its skin to match its background. Dark brown shannies are found amongst brown seaweeds whilst olive green fish are found in green seaweeds. The shanny feeds on small crabs and other crustaceans. They are very slippery fish and they can flip across rocks using their spiny front fins. Female shannies lay their eggs on the underside of rocks where the eggs are guarded by the male fish until they hatch. While they are small, they live at sea but they move to the seashore once they are older.

Gobies are also found on seashores. Their pelvic fins (paired fins at the back of the body) form a sucker that helps them grip to rocks. Gobies feed on shrimps, molluscs, young fish and seaweeds. The common goby is found in estuaries and pools high up on sandy beaches while the rock goby prefers rocky shores.

Be a seashore detective

You can become a seashore detective. First, you will need some equipment. Take this book with you to help you find and identify the animals and seaweeds on the seashore. You will also need a notebook, pencil, magnifying glass, beach shoes and a small net to catch the animals. A small bucket is useful as you can fill it with seawater as a temporary home for the animals you find. Always remember to put back all the animals and seaweeds carefully when you have finished looking at them. You can look at the animals more closely with the magnifying glass when they are in the bucket. A camera can be useful too as you can record your finds. Use your notebook and camera to record the appearance and size of the animal, the

◀ You can spend hours on a beach looking for animals. Remember to keep a watch on the tide and to cover your skin to protect it from the sun.

type of shore and where on the shore that you found it. This will help you to identify it. You will need to wear a pair of beach shoes to protect your feet as you clamber over rocks or gravel. Also a small stick is useful to move seaweed or rocks as you do not know what may be lurking underneath! If you move a stone to look underneath, always roll it back again.

On a rocky shore you can look for animals on the rocks and in the rock pools. On the upper shore, animals will be hiding in small cracks and under seaweeds and stones. There will be larger rock pools lower down the beach and more animals will be in these pools of water.

A sandy beach may look empty but the animals are living in the sand so walk along and look for holes that are entrances to burrows. There is usually a pile of washed up seaweeds and other debris at the high tide mark. This is called the strand line. Here you will find lots of dried seaweeds, egg cases of whelks, the empty egg cases of the dogfish, called a mermaid's purse, cuttlefish bones, crab claws and lots of shells. Birds search the strand line looking for small animals to eat.

▲ *The view on the left shows a rocky shore at high tide when most of the shore is covered by water. The view on the right shows the same shore at low tide when all the shore is exposed, leaving rock pools between the rocks.*

Glossary

Bivalve A mollusc that has two shells hinged together.

Carapace The part of a crab's exoskeleton that covers its back.

Crustacean An animal that has legs that are jointed and a heavy exoskeleton that protects the soft body inside, for example crabs.

Encrusting Forming a thin layer over something.

Estuary The place where a river empties into the sea.

Exoskeleton A hard outer-shell or structure around the outside of an animal such as an insect or crab.

Filter To separate small particles from water.

Frond Name given to the leaf-like structure of seaweeds.

Gill An organ used to breathe under water.

Herbivore An animal that feeds on plant foods.

Holdfast A type of root that attaches a seaweed to a rock.

Microscopic Too small to be seen with the eye and so is studied using a microscope.

Mollusc An animal that usually has a shell and a muscular foot used for moving around.

Mucus A jelly-like substance. Seaweeds produce mucus to help prevent their fronds from losing too much water and drying out.

Nocturnal To be most active at night.

Plankton Microscopic plants and animals that float in the upper layer of seas and lakes.

Predator An animal that hunts and eats other animals.

Radula The tongue of a mollusc which is covered in lots of tiny teeth and used to scrape food.

Rock pool A small pool of water that is trapped between the rocks when the tide goes out.

Regeneration The ability to regrow part of the body, for example starfish can regenerate a missing arm.

Seaweed A plant-like organism that grows in salt water.

Shell The hard outer covering of a mollusc such as a snail or mussel.

Silica A substance found in rocks and sand.

Stipe The stalk-like part of a seaweed, which connects the frond to the holdfast.

Tide The regular rise and fall of sea level on a shore. There are two high tides and two low tides each day.

Further information

Books

Photographic Guide to Sea and Shore Life of Britain and North-west Europe by Ray Gibson, Alex Rogers, Ben Hextall (Oxford University Press, 2001)

Collins Pocket Guide: Seashore by Peter Hayward et al (Collins, 1996)

Michelin Green Guides: Green Guide to Seashore Life of Britain and Europe by Bob Gibbons et al (New Holland Publishers, 2001)

Philip's Guide to Seashores and Shallow Seas of Britain and Europe by Andrew C. Campbell, James Nicholl (Illustrator) (Philip's, 2005)

Life Series: Seaweeds by David N. Thomas (The Natural History Museum, 2002)

Guide to Seashells of the World: A Complete Reference Guide to Shells by A.P.H. Oliver (Philip's, 2004)

Websites

www.national-aquarium.co.uk
Full of information about marine life.

www.habitas.org.uk/marinelife/index.html
Quite a complicated website, but lots of interesting pictures.

Places to visit

London Aquarium, County Hall, Westminster Bridge Road, London SE1 7PB

National Marine Aquarium, Rope Walk, Coxside, Plymouth PL4 0LF

Blue Reef Aquarium, Portsmouth, Newquay and Tynemouth
See fish and other marine animals close-up.

Visit beaches near your home, but check the tide times first as you will want to visit when the tide is out.

Index

Page numbers in **bold** indicate pictures.